IMPROVING EMPLOYEE PERFORMANCE

IMPROVING EMPLOYEE PERFORMANCE

Effective Training Strategies and Techniques

Herman E Zaccarelli

This book is dedicated to Dr and Mrs Lewis J Minor and George and Toodie St Laurent

First published in the United States of America in 1988, entitled *Training Managers to Train*, by Crisp Publications Inc, 95 First Street, Los Altos, California 94022, USA.

This edition first published in Great Britain in 1992 by Kogan Page Ltd, 120 Pentonville Road, London N1 9JN.

British Library Cataloguing in Publication Data

A CIP record for this book is available from the British Library.

ISBN 0-7494-0610-0

Typeset by DP Photosetting, Aylesbury, Bucks
Printed and bound in Great Britain by
Biddles Ltd, Guildford and Kings Lynn

Contents

Preface

Managers at all organisational levels, whether they own their own business or work for someone else, must supervise people. Done correctly, everyone benefits and the manager will receive credit for a job well done. If, on the other hand, employees are not managed effectively, no one will benefit, and the manager will quickly get the blame! The task of directing people at work is not easy because employees, as human beings, are very complex. However, employees cannot perform well at work no matter how hard they try and regardless of how much they want to until they know *what* they are supposed to do and *how* they are supposed to do it. A well-developed training programme addresses both of these issues.

Improving Employee Performance focuses on answering the question: How *exactly* does a manager prepare for, plan, present, and follow up on training programmes designed to produce competent employees? The answer to this question is presented in the following pages.

Training schemes can be fun to develop and to present. And they can make a significant difference to your organisation's success. Readers will find this book easy to read and use. The efforts spent learning about training by putting the basic principles in this book to work can be rewarding to everyone – management, employees, and customers.

About This Book

Learning from this book will be interesting and fun because you are not just going to read it; you are going to use it! You'll be working with a pencil or pen as much as you'll be reading. In the process, you'll learn more because there will be opportunities to apply what you are learning.

This programme is designed for you if:

- You are aspiring to become a manager and want to learn more about the many requirements of managing.
- You are already a manager and want to learn more about training.
- You are a trainer and want to get some ideas about programmes which can be used to help other people learn how to train.
- You are a student and want to learn more about the instructional design aspects of training.

In addition to using this book as you work through it, you will be able to use it later. If you encounter a problem that can be addressed through training while you are at work, this book will provide a review of techniques which will help you to develop and implement training programmes.

Objectives of Improving Employee Performance

An objective states the purpose of training; it tells what the trainer wants to accomplish. A *competence-based* objective states the purpose from the trainee's perspective. It indicates what the trainee is expected to know or be able to do *after* the training is completed.

After reading this book and working through suggested exercises the reader will be able to master the objectives listed below.

Objectives	Page(s)
☐ 1. *Define* a competence-based trainee objective.	8–9
☐ 2. *Know* why training is important from the perspective of both the trainer *and* the trainee.	11–16
☐ 3. *Give* a brief overview of the four basic steps in training programme development and implementation.	21
☐ 4. *Conduct* a position analysis including the development of required analysis forms.	22–30
☐ 5. *State* four uses of a job description.	30
☐ 6. *Develop* training objectives, training plans and training lessons.	33–38
☐ 7. *Select* qualified trainers.	38–39
☐ 8. *List* eight factors to weigh up when considering group or individual training.	41
☐ 9. *Describe* major principles of group training.	40–41
☐ 10. *Design* an on-the-job training programme which incorporates principles in the four-step method.	45–52
☐ 11. *Relate* training evaluation to the training programme objectives.	53–54
☐ 12. *Recite* ten principles of coaching.	55–56
☐ 13. *Design* an induction checklist.	58–60

CHAPTER 1
Why it is Important to Train Employees

A manager is busy and has many things to do. There is only time for the most important, high priority activities.

Training styles

Every manager brings a different personality to training. This individual style, however, must be blended into an effective training format if the outcome is to be successful. Several reasons why training is important regardless of the trainer's style are described below. Tick those with which you agree.

Which of the following would benefit your organisation?

☐ **Saving money.** If employees know how to work the *right* way, costs will be lower; profits will be higher.

☐ **Saving employees.** Employees who know how to work according to their boss's expectations will be less anxious and staff turnover will be reduced.

☐ **Saving customers and making new ones.** Customers are happy when they receive the products/services they expect. Training helps to ensure that this will happen *consistently*.

We hope you ticked *all* the above. Training can provide all these benefits. You, your customers, your employees and your organisation have a lot to gain – and nothing to lose – from using a quality training programme. Which of the following will benefit your organisation?

☐ **Saving time.** – A trained staff will promote efficiency. Both the manager's and the employees' time will be saved.

☐ **Reducing staffing concerns.** Trained employees are better prepared and more eligible for promotion opportunities.

☐ **Saving relationships.** Managers who show their concern for employees with quality training help to motivate them and morale levels are likely to increase.

Training is part of effective supervision

Training is an essential part of effective management and supervision of employees. Employee performance will improve when managers and workers realise the value of training at work and take steps to implement it. Listed below are reminders for the manager about prioritising his own training and that of his employees.

- A manager must do many things at once. All are important. Nothing is more important than training.
- The management of people determines organisational success. Training cannot wait until 'the manager gets around to it' or 'when time permits'.
- Training must receive high priority from management. The highest levels of management must agree about the importance of training and allocate time and resources for it to be done well.
- No manager can train in a vacuum. Top management must endorse the value of training and employees must be convinced of what training will do for them.
- Managers must be effective trainers.

Training know-how is a must for managers

A trainer's work covers a whole spectrum of responsibility from working to budgets to staff training and supervision; from imposing and meeting deadlines to ensuring the consistent quality of the product/service for which they are responsible.

Training helps them to prioritise these responsibilities, allows them to delegate and helps to improve performance.

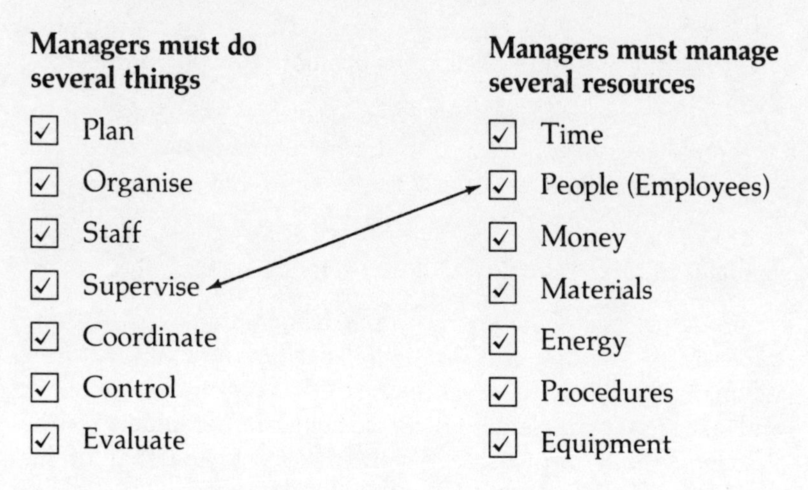

As managers supervise employees they must:

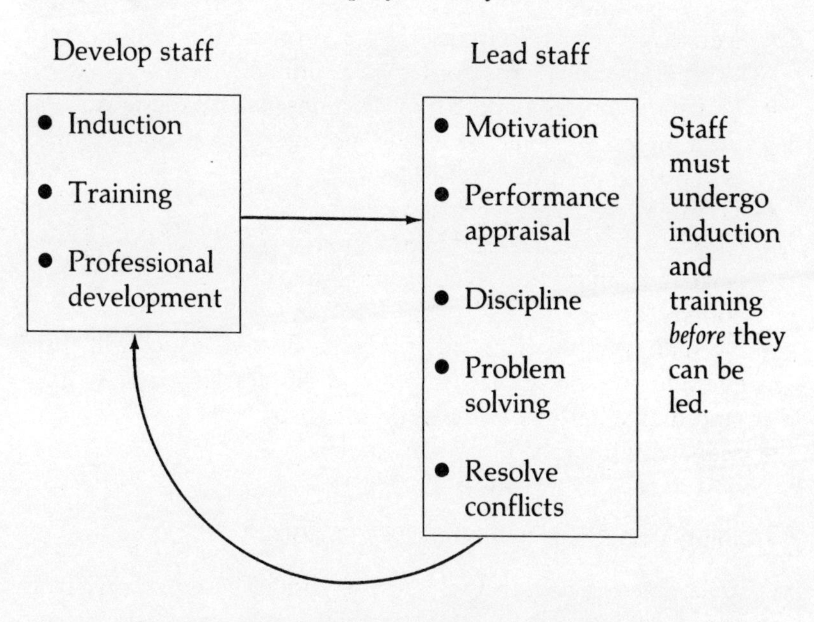

Training is not a luxury for managers . . . it is a necessity!

CHAPTER 2
Employees Benefit From Training

Employees benefit from training. Management's job is to demonstrate how training will help employees. Properly explained, it will be attractive to employees. They will *participate* in training activities. They will receive greater benefits from their training experience. There's an old saying, 'If a trainee hasn't learned it's because the trainer hasn't trained.' Trainees who understand the benefits they can receive from training will *want* to learn.

Tick any of the following you would like to achieve:

☐ Personal knowledge that you are doing a good job.

☐ Wage/salary increase.

☐ No anxiety about performance evaluations.

☐ Fewer customer complaints.

☐ Feeling of being a 'professional'.

☐ Respect/esteem from customers, peers, and your boss.

☐ Promotion.

☐ Freedom from on-the-job accidents.

☐ Increase in tips, perks or benefits (where applicable).

☐ Freedom from boredom at work.

☐ Less tiresome work.

☐ Participation in career development programmes.

- ☐ Knowledge that your job is secure.
- ☐ Better relationship with your manager.
- ☐ Job enjoyment.
- ☐ Good work experience.
- ☐ Less stress.
- ☐ Improved teamwork.
- ☐ More fun on the job.

Guess what? Your employees are likely to have ticked the same things that you did. You may have ticked all the factors. Each one of them is influenced by training.

When can training help?

We've painted a bright picture of training. Done effectively, it's good for everyone – the manager, employees, and the customers. In other words, any organisation will benefit from a good training programme.

Will training solve all the problems of the business? Will all situations be improved by training? The answer to both questions is *No*.

When *will* training help?

Training will only help to resolve problems when employees want to learn (have the proper attitude) and when job knowledge is lacking or inadequate. When these two factors are not present, other management solutions are more appropriate.

Assessing when training is appropriate

Imagine a situation in which the manager thinks about a particular employee in terms of perceived attitude (good or poor) and level of job knowledge (high or low).

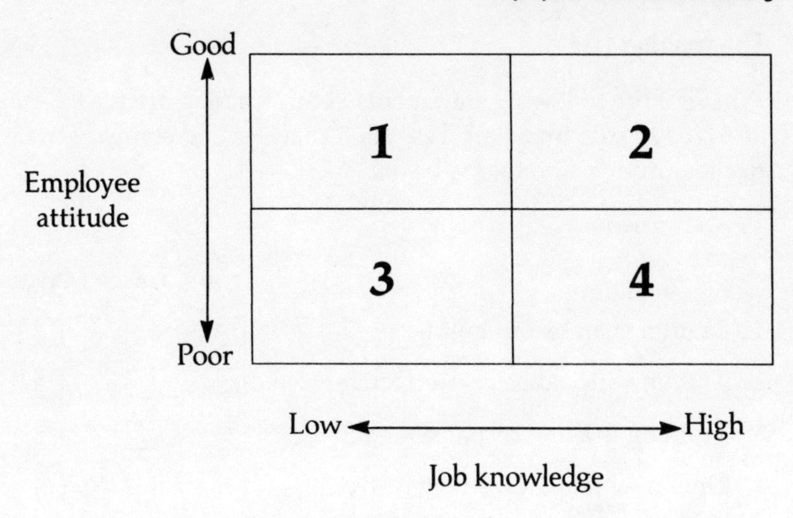

Let's look at each of the possibilities:

Box 1 (Good Attitude/Low Job Knowledge). An employee with a good attitude and low level of job knowledge *can* be helped dramatically by training.

Box 2 (Good Attitude/High Job Knowledge). In this situation training will help provided there is adequate time, etc.

Box 3 (Poor Attitude/Low Job Knowledge). In this situation personnel action (such as reassigning duties) may be most appropriate. Training is unlikely to help if the person who needs training is not interested in learning.

Box 4 (Poor Attitude/High Job Knowledge). This employee could do the job with the proper attitude, but without it, training will not reduce the problem.

Training works when the employee wants to learn and has a positive attitude but does not know how to do the work required.

What training isn't

So it is clear that training doesn't work in every situation. It works best for employees who are interested in learning the knowledge and skills required to do the job.

The training test

Which of the following statements about training are true, false, or partially true (maybe)? Tick your answers and compare them to the author's statements below.

	True	False	Maybe
1. Training can be difficult.	☐	☐	☐
2. Training should be cost-effective.	☐	☐	☐
3. Training is a line responsibility.	☐	☐	☐
4. Only new employees benefit from training.	☐	☐	☐
5. Training can modify an employee's attitudes.	☐	☐	☐
6. Training is best when objectives involve increasing/changing, knowledge/skill levels.	☐	☐	☐
7. Training should be done when time permits.	☐	☐	☐
8. Training for problem resolution is different from teaching a new employee job skills.	☐	☐	☐

Learn the training basics

This guide will present the basics of training. These basics should be used consistently:

- During the induction of new employees
- To upgrade the knowledge/skills of existing staff
- To provide long-term professional development
- To resolve operating problems.

Once the basics of training are mastered they can be used any time that training activities are being used. Training should *not* be difficult for those who complete this book. Readers will learn how to define jobs and acquire the knowledge and skills necessary to be a good trainer.

Are you concerned about the answer to question 1 on the Training Test (page 18: Training can be difficult)? We answered this question 'yes' because training *is* difficult for many people. It takes a special effort to define *how* jobs should be done and to plan the subsequent training. It is also difficult because a trainer must have knowledge and skills which go beyond common sense and on-the-job experience.

Check your answers.

Author response

1. True. Training can be difficult; it takes skilful planning to implement a quality training programme.
2. True. Training *must* be cost-effective or it should not be undertaken.
3. True. Line managers, not those in the personnel office, should be ultimately responsible for training.
4. False. *All* employees benefit from training.

5/6. Maybe. It is difficult to modify attitudes. Training is most typically helpful in influencing knowledge/skill levels.

7. False. Training is too important to do only when time permits; it must receive priority.
8. False. The basic training techniques are the same regardless of the purpose.

Training basics are universal

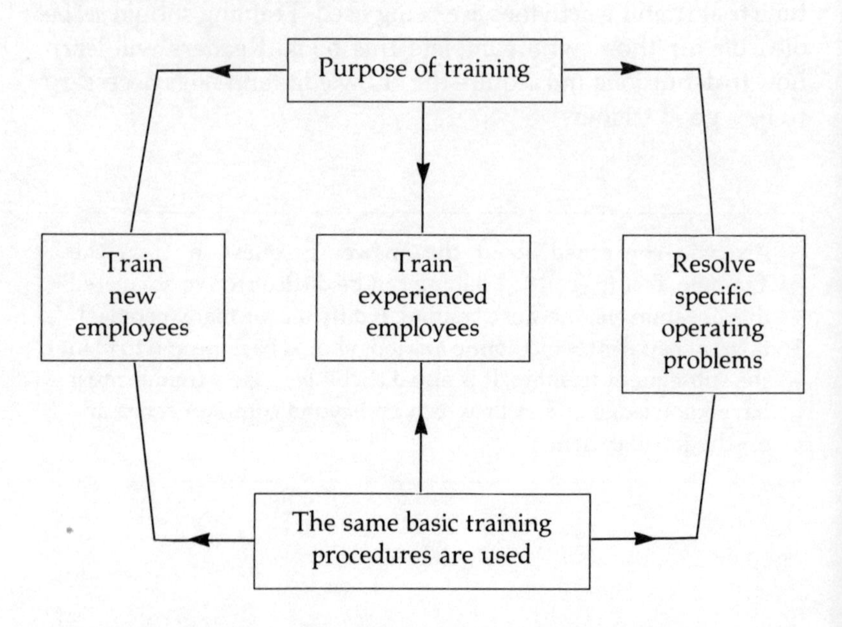

The basic procedures for effective training (regardless of the depth of the training) involves a four-step method. This method will be explained in the second part of this book.

CHAPTER 3
The Four Steps of Training

Regardless of the purpose of the training programme (to teach new employees, to upgrade knowledge/skills of experienced employees, or to resolve operating problems) or the type of training (individual or group) four basic steps are involved. They are:

Step 1. Define how the job should be done
Step 2. Plan the training
Step 3. Present the training
Step 4. Evaluate the training

Employees should not be trained to do a job until the *correct* way to do the work has been defined. This step is often omitted. Training activities need to be planned. Planning is often non-existent or inadequate. Professional trainers know that significant preparation is required *before* training begins.

STEP 1
Define How the Job Should Be Done

The first step in training is to define how the job you will train others for should be done. This process involves developing a *position analysis*. A trainer must know how the job should be done before the 'best' way can be taught.

The following activities are required to develop a position analysis:

- Develop a list of tasks
  A task is a single element/activity of a job. Jobs are typically composed of several different specific tasks.
- Define the task
  A description of *exactly* how a task should be performed.
- Determine the required quality level for each task.
- Construct a job description.

Trainers know that a position analysis is an important first step in training. They also know, however, that the process used must be simple, practical and efficient.

Why a position analysis?

Tick each of the following statements whether true or false as they apply to your organisation.

	True	False
1. All employees in the same position perform each task of their job in the same way.	☐	☐
2. Every supervisor for a specific area of responsibility would give the same explanation of how each task should be done.	☐	☐
3. It takes different employees approximately the same amount of time to perform a specific task.	☐	☐
4. All employees use the same process/ procedures to perform identical tasks.	☐	☐
5. Customers compliment your organisation about the consistency of employee task procedures they encounter.	☐	☐
6. Similar quality standards are consistently attained by all employees.	☐	☐
7. The definition of what constitutes 'good' performance is understood by all members of staff and is used as the basis for training, supervision and performance appraisals.	☐	☐
8. Job descriptions accurately portray the work to be done.	☐	☐

If you answered honestly, it is probable you answered that all statements are false. If you think about each question, however, you probably recognise that in an *ideal* organisation, most questions could be answered true.

> When job tasks are performed with consistency by employees, quality standards can be defined; time and cost requirements can be established; and guidelines for performance evaluation criteria can be developed.

Position analysis: the four activities

1. Develop a list of tasks
2. Define a task
3. Determine required quality levels
4. Design a job description

1. Develop a list of tasks

The first activity for a quality position analysis is the development of a task list. This list will specify all job elements which a person (such as a sales clerk, computer operator or maintenance supervisor) must do to satisfy the job requirements of that position. Once a manager/trainer identifies and lists these activities, the outlines of a training programme will have been defined.

How is a task list developed?

- Think about the required tasks to perform a specific job.
- Observe employees in that job. Observe what they do.
- Discuss with employees the tasks they do and ask their opinions about which are the most important and why.
- Ask other supervisors to identify tasks which their subordinates perform in similar job situations.
- Study the job description to see how accurately it reflects the objectives of the specific job.

Sample task list

Position: ______________________________

Tasks required to perform in this position (listed by priority):

1. ______________________________
2. ______________________________
3. ______________________________
4. ______________________________
5. ______________________________

All significant tasks (which an employee working in a specific position must do) should be listed. For example, a sales clerk may, as part of the job:

1. operate the cash register correctly for each transaction (daily)
2. complete a daily sales report to the specifications required (daily)
3. attend to the needs of customers (daily)
4. conduct inventory counts (weekly)
5. vacuum the carpet (daily).

Once all basic tasks have been identified, a person with training responsibilities will know what a *new* sales clerk must accomplish. To be successful, a training programme must present all the necessary information to allow a newly employed sales clerk to understand and perform the job to the level of quality expected. See pages 67–68 to apply what you have learned.

2. Define a task

The second activity to develop a position analysis is to design a method to break down each task. This breakdown answers the question, 'How *exactly* should a task be performed?' It should tell the 'how, when and what' of each task and specify any required equipment, supplies, or procedures that are needed.

How is a task breakdown developed? The same process used to develop a task list can be employed:

- A manager/trainer should think about the preferred way to perform a task.
- Employees who do the work should be observed and consulted.
- Supervisors of those who do similar tasks should be asked to explain how to ideally complete each task.

It is likely that a careful analysis of how work is currently done will yield excellent ideas about how it can be improved. While a new way is not always better, there are often better ways to accomplish any task.

Sample task breakdown

Position: ____________________ **Task:** ____________________

The procedures to complete this task include:

Step	Process	Equipment/ Supplies	Time Requirements	Other
1.				
2.				
3.				
4.				
5.				

A task breakdown describes, in sequence, what employees must do in order to perform a task correctly. Consider, for example, a sales clerk operating a cash register. Operating instructions provided by the manufacturer of the equipment might be an excellent starting point. These can then be integrated into the specific job requirements.

Or, how exactly should inventory counts be taken? What considerations are necessary when approaching a customer, etc? The answers to *these* questions cannot be supplied in a manufacturer's instruction book. The procedures which evolve to answer questions such as these can be very beneficial *even before training activities begin*. See pages 68–69 to practise breaking down one of your tasks at work.

3. Determine required quality levels

The third activity in position analysis is the consideration of the quality level required for the task. What must be done to ensure that these quality standards are met? Today everyone is talking about the need for improved quality. Studies show that customers are willing to pay extra for quality service. On the other hand, businesses lose customers when quality is lacking. Customers have long memories when quality problems occur.

Managers must design quality standards into the way work is done. The training programme must stress quality and show each employer why it is essential.

Trainers must:

- Ensure that the task breakdown will yield output that meets or exceeds quality standards.
- Consistently stress the importance of quality as an integral part of each task.
- Show how quality standards are built into work output.
- Identify those products/services which do not meet quality standards and correct them.

Trainees may not be able to attain required quality levels immediately. Time is needed to build skills necessary to meet quality standards. Employees should be able to identify quality requirements by the time training is completed. They should also be given a time by which the desired quality levels need to be achieved.

Quality standards test

Tick the following statements which are true in your organisation:

	True
1. Quality standards have been established for all activities undertaken by employees in all positions.	☐
2. Quality of work output is a significant factor in employee appraisals.	☐
3. Customer complaints about quality problems are *extremely* rare.	☐

4. Quality is just as important as quantity when tasks are performed. ☐

5. Quality standards are consistently measured and reported on. ☐

6. Management's philosophy and expectations about maintaining quality standards are well known. ☐

7. Employee training programmes emphasise quality requirements as skills that are taught. ☐

8. Employees are rewarded by meeting/exceeding quality goals. ☐

How many did you tick as true? Any that were not ticked need immediate attention.

Think about the products and services you purchase as a consumer. What makes you happy? Disappointed? What factors in your personal situation are applicable to the products/services provided by your organisation? What can you learn from this analysis? How can you apply your own perceptions of quality to the way things are done by your employees?

4. Design a job description

The final activity in the position analysis process is to develop a job description. This important personnel management tool has many uses. A trainer with a current job description has a head start to ensure that employees recruited and selected have the appropriate training activities.

Large organisations typically have personnel departments to help recruit employees. It is very important that operating departments provide the personnel department with updated job descriptions. If this does not occur, there may be surprises when a newly employed worker discovers what the job really involves.

Sample job description

Position: ______________ Date of last revision: __/__/__

Level: __________

1. This position reports to: ______________________
2. This position supervises: ______________________
3. Basic tasks for this position include:

   A ______________________

   B ______________________

   C ______________________

   D ______________________

   E ______________________

   F ______________________

   G ______________________

   H ______________________

4. Knowledge of equipment required includes:

   ____

5. Personal qualifications judged most important for this job are:

   ____

6. Quality standards for this position ensure:

   ____

7. Description of other important aspects of this position are:

   ____

8. Etc.

   ____

This is a very simple job description. Many job descriptions are more complex. Only the most important tasks should be included on the sheet. Personal qualities are sometimes included in a separate 'job specification' sheet. We have combined them here.

Uses of a job description

Once developed, a job description can be used for many purposes, some of which are listed below.

- To inform applicants being recruited about important aspects of the job
- To indicate the outlines of job requirements to be addressed during training
- As a management tool to help supervise employees
- To assist in employee appraisal (employees should be evaluated on how well they do the work described in the job description).

Job descriptions are useful *after* an employee has been taken on, as well as when applicants are being recruited. Try to answer the following questions. See opposite the answers suggested by the author to judge how you got on.

1. How do job descriptions relate to training programmes?

____

____

____

2. What can happen if job descriptions are not kept up to date?

____

____

____

3. What is the difference between a job description and a performance appraisal?

____

____

Author response

1. Job descriptions specify tasks for which training is necessary. They also help to ensure that qualified employees are taken on.
2. Problems will occur when job descriptions do not accurately describe the work that needs to be done.
3. Job descriptions describe tasks which are part of a position. Performance appraisals are methods used by management to evaluate how well a job is being performed.

See pages 69–70 if you need more practice with job descriptions.

STEP 2
Plan the Training

We have now learned the importance of developing a position analysis. As a result, a manager/trainer should know all major aspects of the job that need to be done. Training based on the position analysis must (a) address all tasks, (b) teach the correct procedures, and (c) determine the required quality levels.

The second step in training is planning. Some individuals underestimate the importance of this step (What is there to plan? We do the work every day and should be able to show someone how to do it. Time saved in planning can be spent in training). *Failure* to plan for training activities could mean your training efforts will fail.

Why proper planning is required

Think about training programmes in which you've been involved. Some may be currently used in your organisation. Did any of the following occur? If so, tick the appropriate box.

1. The trainer 'forgot' that training was to take place. ☐
2. As a trainee, you were uncertain about what you needed to learn. ☐
3. The training was often interrupted because of outside priorities. ☐
4. The quality of training was lowered by the lack of supplies or unavailable equipment. ☐

5. The procedures taught by the trainer were not consistent with: ☐

   what the written or audio/visual materials said to do ☐

   what others told you to do ☐

   what you *saw* others do. ☐

6. The training was not well organised; for example, procedures were taught out of sequence. ☐

7. The trainer did not seem to care about training you. ☐

8. The trainer was ineffective because of attitude or a lack of knowledge. ☐

9. There were no written or other materials to help you learn. ☐

10. Training was done 'only when there was time.' ☐

> If you have had first-hand experience with any of the problems listed above, *you now know why training is important!*

Planning for training

1. Consider training objectives
2. Develop a training plan
3. Design a training lesson
4. Select the trainer(s)
5. Prepare the trainer(s)

1. Consider training objectives

The first concern when planning is to consider the training objectives. You can't plan a programme until you first know what the training is to accomplish. At the beginning of this book we stated some objectives. These were set out in terms of what you (the reader) should know or be able to do after you complete this guide. As the trainer, when you plan a training programme, it is equally important to consider what the trainees should know or be able to do after the training is complete.

Training objectives should be attainable. Both trainer and trainees will be frustrated if impossible goals are set. Objectives should also be measurable. At the end of the training programme, the trainer and trainees should be able to discuss how well the goals were met. Objectives also help during the evaluation stage which will be discussed later. The training programme is successful if the objectives are achieved.

Training objectives must be attainable and measurable

Which of the following training programme objectives are attainable and measurable? Compare your answers with those of the author opposite.

	Attainable	Measurable
1. There will never be any accidents.	☐	☐
2. Accident rates can be reduced.	☐	☐
3. Employees will always have the proper attitude about safety.	☐	☐
4. Employees can be taught to operate the equipment according to procedures in the task breakdown.	☐	☐
5. Employees will appreciate the need to operate equipment safely.	☐	☐
6. Employees can be trained to complete an accident follow-up report correctly.	☐	☐
7. Employees can be trained to perform each task for their position correctly.	☐	☐

Author response

1. This is probably not attainable but is measurable. Accidents can be reduced but not eliminated (due to the human factor).
2. This is probably attainable and can be measured by determining if the rate after training is lower than before training.
3. Attitudes are difficult to measure; this is probably not an attainable objective.
4. This is attainable and measurable.
5. Same answer as question 3.
6. This is attainable and measurable. The definition of 'correctly' refers to procedures outlined in the job breakdown for each task.
7. Both attainable and measurable.

2. Develop a training plan

Once attainable and measurable training objectives have been considered, a training plan can be developed. This planning tool provides a step-by-step written document for others to follow. A training plan can be for either a *complete* training programme or for just one task.

3. Design a training lesson

Once a training plan outlining general programme requirements has been developed, a trainer will need to concentrate on specific segments of that plan. This is done with the use of a training lesson. Generally, there is one training lesson for each training session. (If ten sessions are planned, ten training lessons are developed.)

A training lesson does several things. It:

- provides a content outline for the session
- suggests activities/specific instructions which will help to make training easier
- defines suggested time to be spent on each segment within the session.

Sample training plan

Session	Date	Time	Employees involved	Training objective	Training site	Trainer(s)	Equipment or supplies	Method/ Lesson
1	8/6	8.00–10.00	JH/JS	1, 2	Lunch room	Jim	OH projector	Lecture 1
2	15/6	9.00–10.00	JH/JS	3, 4	Sales Office	Jim	Video	Individual 2
3	22/6	7.30–9.30	JH/JS	5, 6	Sales Office	Jim	Blackboard	Lecture 3
4	etc							
10	8/12	10.00–11.00	JH/JS	19, 20	Client's Office	Jim	None	Individual 10

Training plans outline a broad schedule. General plans are normally designed for several sessions. See page 71 to have a go at working with a training plan.

Task breakdowns are used for training lessons

If the specific training session is designed to teach employees how to perform a task, the task breakdown becomes a major part of the training lesson. An important job planning tool becomes an important training tool!

Training lessons organise training sessions

What *exactly* does the trainer do during a training session? How much time should be allowed? These are questions answered by a training lesson. Consider the sample below:

Sample Training Lesson

Training topic: Operate company cash register properly

Objective(s): Once training is completed, a sales clerk should know how to operate the cash register to company specifications.

Content of session	Suggested activities	Time
1. Procedures for cash register operation are found in the operations manual for the machine and augmented by company manuals for special purchases.	1. Provide a copy of instructions from the manual.	N/A
	2. Talk through the operating techniques.	10 minutes
	3. Use training software, work through several examples of machine operation.	40 minutes
	4. Review what has been learned by allowing trainees to demonstrate understanding with 'real life' examples.	10 minutes per trainee

The content column may include actual information (such as the task breakdown) or information the instructor has adapted from other resources such as books or magazines. Suggested activities should allow trainees to participate in the training programme. Try developing your own training lesson on page 72.

4. Select the trainer(s)

Who is going to train? Who is a good communicator and has the necessary knowledge/skill to train? What should the trainer do to get the trainees ready for the training?

Who will be a good trainer?

Not everyone will be an effective trainer. Which of the following characteristics/factors do you think are important to consider when selecting a trainer? Tick those which you think are important, then compare your ideas with those of the author opposite.

1. The best trainers will be found in the personnel department. ☐
2. The most experienced employee will automatically be the best trainer. ☐
3. The trainer must have an interest in training. ☐
4. The trainer should have a sense of humour. ☐
5. The trainer must be a good communicator. ☐
6. The trainer must have patience. ☐
7. The trainer must be a manager. ☐
8. The trainer must have the time to train. ☐
9. The trainer must have the respect of colleagues. ☐
10. The trainer must be 'higher up' in the organisation. ☐
11. The trainer must be enthusiastic. ☐
12. The trainer must be the person who developed the training plan and training lesson. ☐

13. The trainer must personally know how to do every task that is required of someone in the position being trained. ☐

5. Prepare the trainer(s)

Training is one of the most important things any organisation does. We have discussed how to plan for training. This concern must carry through to the trainer. When a busy supervisor or employee is asked to provide on-the-job training for a new staff member but is not given release time or told how to train, problems will result.

What about preparing trainees?

Trainees must be considered. They must be prepared for the experience. To prepare trainees, consider ways to:

- Reduce anxieties by telling trainees what the training will involve
- Emphasise that trainee concerns will be addressed
- Inform trainees that training will directly relate to the work they were employed to do
- Indicate that efforts will be made to keep the training experience enjoyable and worthwhile
- Let trainees know the basis on which they will be evaluated.

Author response

The following characteristics are important in a trainer: 3, 4, 5, 6, 8, 9, 11.

Number 13 is incorrect because different trainers can be used to teach employees different tasks.

STEP 3
Present the Training

The third step in the training process becomes important once work procedures have been defined and *after* the training is planned. The training must be presented to the trainee(s). No doubt, the decision to use group or individual methods will have been addressed as the training was planned.

There is a wide range of useful training methods. These include:

- *Lectures* – where a trainer talks to the trainees. Videos, overhead projectors, slides, films, etc can supplement the lecture.
- *Role-playing* – trainees act out situations after learning basic principles.
- *Case studies* – trainees read, analyse and discuss real life situations.
- *Demonstration* – a trainer (or other party) shows the trainees how to do something.
- *Self-study materials* – such as this book.

These can be used for both group and individual training. There are also other types of individual training. However, the most common method, and that which will be reviewed at length in this book, is on-the-job training.

Group or individual training

What factors should be considered when deciding which type of training – group or individual – to use? Compare your beliefs with those of the author at the foot of the page. Tick the type of training which is generally best for each factor.

Situation	Best training method: Group	Individual
1. The same information needs to be presented to several people.	☐	☐
2. The primary purpose of training is to present a wide range of extensive details.	☐	☐
3. When time is limited and several trainees must be trained.	☐	☐
4. When trainees' experience and background are similar.	☐	☐
5. When cost is a consideration.	☐	☐
6. When training needs to involve the trainee personally.	☐	☐
7. When highly specialised training is required.	☐	☐
8. Training that requires the least amount of training.	☐	☐

Group training: some important principles

Regardless of the group training method selected, some important principles should be addressed before the programme is planned and implemented. These principles centre around the need for a trainer to practise the 'art and science' of training.

Author response

Group training: 1, 3, 4, 5
Individual training: 2, 6, 7
Number 8: neither; both methods require extensive planning.

Concepts useful in group training are:

- Planning principles
- Implementing principles
- Evaluating principles

Most successful training programmes use both group and individual activities. Regardless of the type of programme, the principles are the same. Training cannot be successful if the basic principles shown above are not incorporated into the programme.

Which of these factors are true about group training?
Tick each of the following statements as either true or false. Compare your answers with those of the author opposite.

	True	False
1. Group training programmes do not require a statement of objectives because each trainee is likely to finish training at a different skill level.	☐	☐
2. The results of group training should be evaluated when the training is completed as well as afterwards, when trainees return to the job.	☐	☐
3. Rehearsals of group training activities are unnecessary. Spontaneous presentations are best.	☐	☐
4. Training presentations are important but the training environment is not.	☐	☐
5. If hand-out materials are used, it is unnecessary for a trainer to provide an oral overview of the programme when it begins.	☐	☐

	True	False
6. If training is being conducted to resolve a problem, both the problem and the results of the solution should be discussed beforehand.	☐	☐
7. Participants in group training are more likely to resist change than those given individual training.	☐	☐
8. If a trainer is effective, each participant in the group training is likely to react the same way during training.	☐	☐
9. Good trainers will adapt their style to the needs of the group.	☐	☐
10. It is generally unwise to ask questions of trainees unless a trainer is concerned about 'filling' time.	☐	☐

On-the-job training

On-the-job training is the most popular training method in small organisations. It is a great method if done correctly. Many managers believe on-the-job training is the best method because (a) it is simple and fast, (b) no planning is required, and (c) it is a method anybody can use.

People who believe these things about on-the-job training are wrong! The method *is* great – but not for these reasons. On-the-job training *is* simple, but only if extensive planning has been done. It is not fast, because time for planning is necessary. The statement that 'anybody can train' using this method is a myth. The same concerns about trainer selection and the need for pre-

Author response

The answers to questions 2, 6 and 9 are true; all other answers are false.

training preparation apply to on-the-job training as well as group training. Before discussing details of on-the-job training, it is important to understand that this method can only be effective when basic training principles are employed. If they are not, training time will be wasted.

On-the-job training: what you should know

Before learning the details about on-the-job training there is some basic information you should know. Each of the following statements about on-the-job training is *true*. Tick those you intend to incorporate in your training procedures:

Pre-planning is necessary. Task lists, task breakdowns, performance standards, training plans and training lessons must be developed before on-the-job training can be used to train new employees. ☐

Trainer selection is important. The trainer must want to train, have adequate job knowledge and understand and use basic training principles. ☐

Written materials such as task breakdowns, operating procedure manuals and handbooks can be helpful to reinforce what trainees learn. ☐

Time for training must be provided. It is usually not adequate to simply allow a trainee to 'tag along' with a more experienced employee as work is performed. ☐

Before demonstrating a work task, it is essential to prepare the work area, collect all appropriate tools, supplies and any other necessary items. ☐

Evaluation is an integral part of on-the-job training. This should be considered as the programme is planned. Some evaluation is necessary both as the programme evolves and at the time of its completion. ☐

Even if a supervisor delegates on-the-job training to a subordinate, it is important for the supervisor to keep up with training progress. This can be done by interviewing the trainer and trainee and closely observing the trainee as initial work activities are performed. ☐

On-the-job training time should not be wasted teaching tasks an employee already understands. An initial study of the task list along with a demonstration of work required for some tasks can clear the way to emphasise activities with which the trainee is unfamiliar. ☐

Four-step, on-the-job training method

1. Preparation
2. Presentation
3. Demonstration
4. Follow-up

1. Preparation

The first step in on-the-job training involves preparation. This step is the most important and often the most overlooked. Simply stated, a trainer does not just 'begin training'. A wide range of activities must be carried out to help ensure that training will be successful. Considering the impact that employees have on customers, it is easy to justify careful planning.

We will discuss each step in on-the-job training in the following pages. This exercise will first identify an important training principle. Next, you will be asked to recall your personal experiences with on-the-job training programmes. Finally, you will consider the negative implications that can arise if training principles are not incorporated. Take time to complete these exercises carefully. After completing the work sheet you will have a greater knowledge of the 'mechanics' of developing, implementing and evaluating an on-the-job training programme.

On-the-job training: preparation

Complete the following exercise. In Column 1 indicate whether the factor noted was addressed in the last on-the-job training programme you attended. In Column 2 think about the problem(s), if any, that can occur if the factor is not used.

Training concept/factor	True in your most recent on-the-job training?		Problem(s) if not used
	Yes	No	
1. Before training began you knew what you were to learn and how long the training would last.			
2. A written task breakdown was used.			
3. The work area was ready and all equipment supplies were present before training began.			
4. You were made comfortable before the training began. There was little stress, anxiety, or pressure in the training environment.			
5. You were given a chance to show you knew about selected tasks before training began, so you could learn only those activities with which you were familiar.			
6. The trainer began each session by telling you what you were supposed to learn.			
7. The trainer had an effective way of evaluating whether you had learned each activity.			
8. You consistently observed 'the right way' being used by other employees once the training session was completed.			

2. Presentation

The second step in on-the-job training involves presentation to the trainee. This step should be easy if the trainer is prepared. This step is more than simply showing an employee how the work should be done. Rather, the trainer must have adequate time to explain to the trainee what must be done while carefully demonstrating the 'whats and whys' of each procedure.

Many managers make the mistake of throwing a new employee into the new work setting without some initial training. They feel this technique hastens learning, since the trainee will have to 'do the work or else'. This is usually not a good technique. Anxiety and stress can make the initial work experience difficult for a new employee. Product quality and/or customer service can be affected. Your customers are not paying a reduced price when they are handled by a trainee. They should consistently receive the quality of the product/service which you promise. This cannot be done when a trainee learns 'at the expense' of the customer. Some training must be done *before* the trainee is put into a position where his or her output will reach the customer.

On-the-job training: presentation

Complete the exercise below. In the first column indicate whether the training concept/factor was addressed in the last programme you attended as a trainee. In Column 2 think about problem(s), if any, created if the factor is not used.

Training concept/factor	True in your most recent on-the-job training?		Problem(s) if not used
	Yes	No	
1. Did the trainer explain each task to you before it was demonstrated?			
2. Did the trainer seem to enjoy and want to undertake the training?			
3. Did the trainer ask you questions and urge you to ask questions as the initial presentation evolved?			
4. Did each activity seem organised? Did it follow procedures written in a task breakdown?			
5. Did you receive the 'right' amount of training in each session? (Could you have learned more or was too much crammed into the time?)			
6. Was the training you received accurate and simple?			
7. Was the training of interest to you? Were there things that the trainer could have done to make it more interesting?			
8. Could you tell that the trainer had done effective planning and had experience presenting this part of the training programme?			

3. Demonstration

The third step in on-the-job training is demonstration. During this step the trainee should be allowed to show the trainer what has been learned. Done effectively, this step involves more than a trainer simply allowing the trainee to work alone and returning later to check performance. Instead, a trainer should closely observe the trainee and provide immediate feedback (positive reinforcement or corrective action help) to help the trainee apply what has been learned.

By now, you probably have noticed that the recommended approach to on-the-job training is different from those with which you have been involved. Can you see why the initial statements about the myths of on-the-job training (little time required, no preparation needed, 'anyone' can train, etc) are untrue? On-the-job training presents a powerful method to teach your employees what they need to know, but these results can only happen when the programme is designed and implemented correctly.

On-the-job training: demonstration

Complete the exercise below. In Column 1 indicate whether the factor noted in the training/concept factor was addressed in the last training programme you attended. In Column 2 think about problem(s), if any, which can be created if the factor is not used.

Training concept/factor	True in your most recent on-the-job training?		Problem(s) if not used
	Yes	No	
1. Did the trainer ask you to describe each activity as you initially performed it?			
2. Did the trainer have you demonstrate tasks?			
3. If you made errors, did the trainer promptly indicate what they were, explain exactly what was wrong and why it was wrong?			
4. If errors were made in your demonstration, did the trainer get upset and blame you for the error?			
5. If errors were made during your demonstration, did the trainer demonstrate the correct way and then allow you to practise the correct method?			
6. Did the trainer congratulate you when you did the work correctly?			
7. Did the trainer explain how the task you demonstrated was part of your training programme?			
8. Did the trainer use a questioning process to help assess whether you knew why work was being done in a specified way?			
9. Did you have opportunities to demonstrate your learning in a situation which would not have a direct impact upon customers?			

4. Follow-up

The final step in on-the-job training involves follow-up. Some managers and trainers omit this step. If the trainee has properly demonstrated the activity, why is follow-up necessary? Over time, trainees forget the required work procedures. They may have discovered short-cuts that are not better methods than those presented during training. These are examples of when the trainer must, after observation, provide corrective action to 'get trainees back on the right track'.

Follow-up involves evaluation. Is the trainee able to do the work in the correct manner? If the correct procedure is defined (a task breakdown is used for this purpose) and if the correct procedure is taught, the trainer should be able to confirm that training has been successful. Notice, however, if either of these steps is omitted (the 'correct' method is not defined or taught) training will be ineffective and the fault will lie with the trainer – not the trainee.

On-the-job training: follow-up

Complete the exercise below. In Column 1 indicate whether the training concept/factor was addressed in the last training programme you attended. In Column 2 think about the problem(s), if any, which can be created if the factor is not used.

Training concept/factor	True in your most recent on-the-job training?		Problem(s) if not used
	Yes	No	
1. Did the trainer provide any follow-up evaluation?			
2. Did the trainer encourage you to ask questions after the training was completed?			
3. Did you know who to ask for follow-up help, if any was needed?			
4. Did the trainer/manager conduct follow-up observations of your work?			
5. Were you provided with encouragement when observations indicated the work was being done correctly?			
6. Were you asked for ideas about how the job might be improved?			
7. Were you asked about ways the training programme might be improved?			
8. Did you feel positive about the training experience?			
9. Was the training experience related to the work you did immediately after training?			
10. Would more or different training have been more effective?			

STEP 4

Training Evaluation

We have indicated that there are four steps involved in training:

Step 1: Define the job
Step 2: Plan the training: think about objectives
Step 3: Present the training: group or individual
Step 4: Evaluate the training: think about the objectives.

We have now reached the point of discussing Step 4 (Evaluation). The need for this step has already been emphasised; our job is now to reinforce how important it is.

Why evaluate?

All trainers need to learn if their training has been successful. If it has, the subject matter, approach and method may be used for additional training efforts. If it has not, current trainees may need additional training and future programmes may need to include different subject matter and/or use different training methods or techniques.

Principles of training evaluation

The following list indicates some important concepts of training evaluation. Tick those concepts you use in your training programmes. Carefully consider the other concepts, they may help you more effectively evaluate the worth of your training efforts.

1. Evaluation efforts must address the extent to which *measurable* objectives stated at the beginning of the training are attained. ☐
2. Evaluation must focus on: ☐

   training methods ☐

   training content ☐

   training environment ☐
3. Trainees can be *asked* about training experiences. ☐
4. Trainees can be *observed* to assess training effectiveness. ☐
5. Trainees can be *tested* to measure knowledge gained. (A *pre-test* about subject matter can be given before the training begins; a *post-test* comprising the same questions is given after training is completed.) ☐
6. Trainers must realise that new techniques should be used if training evaluation consistently identifies problems. ☐
7. Evaluation done before the conclusion of training can help a trainer to identify areas where changes in training can be helpful. ☐
8. As training programmes are planned, trainers should consistently think about how they will be evaluated. ☐
9. Trainers should use *results* of training evaluation to assess the cost-effectiveness of training efforts. ☐

Coaching: follow-up is critical

Is the training programme complete once the evaluation has been done? The answer is *No!* When does training stop and normal supervision begin? This question, while perhaps more one of language than substance, introduces us to the concept of coaching.

Coaching is the ongoing reinforcement of the positive aspects of training. It involves:

- Focusing on special problems which must be resolved
- Maintaining open and effective communication with employees
- Providing employees with ongoing opportunities for professional growth.

Coaching activities involve communicating with employees about work-related problems. Both the manager and the trainee will engage in a problem-solving process. Their relationship should improve, work should be done more effectively, and the customers should be better served. Good coaching should always be friendly and practical.

Coaching principles

Try to practise the following coaching principles during training sessions you conduct. Tick the concepts you routinely use and make a serious effort to incorporate others into your future sessions.

1. Allow employees to become involved in the development of work procedures which they will use. ☐
2. Permit employees to evaluate their work and make recommendations for improvement. ☐
3. Undertake corrective action interviews in private. ☐
4. Evaluate the work of each employee by comparing their performance against task breakdowns and job descriptions. ☐
5. Concentrate on the procedures taught during training and the way the trainee works on the job as the evaluation is done. ☐
6. Establish time frames for corrective action. ☐

7. Have the manager indicate his or her ideas about how work performance can be improved. ☐
8. Establish a schedule for subsequent review of work performance. ☐
9. Allow ample time for 'trained' employees to develop skills and/or build speed. ☐
10. Use open-ended questions to encourage each trainee to explain problems which they have encountered. ☐

Induction: start of training

A new applicant's first impressions about his or her job can make all the difference. The foundation for attitudes which may stay in place as long as that employee remains at work are established during induction.

Selection and turnover: a 'chicken and egg' problem?

Many organisations experience high levels of employee turnover. New employees are more likely to leave than long-term workers. What does it mean when there are high turnover levels? Were 'bad' employee selection decisions made? Were 'poor' employee management practices undertaken *after* the new employee began work? Are both factors common reasons for turnover? Regardless of whether the problem rests with selection, or supervision, or both, the result is the same. When an employee leaves, staffing expenses are incurred. Also service to customers is likely to decline. An employee's initial impressions of the company are important. Don't destroy all the work done in bringing a 'good' employee to the job by 'putting off' that employee through improper induction and poor training.

Induction typically involves providing new employees with information that all employees, regardless of position, must know: the mission and objectives of the company; the policies and procedures that are applicable to all staff members; where things are located, etc.

Induction can be formal or informal. It can be done through

discussion or the use of other media. Regardless of the methods used for induction, these programmes must be carefully planned to ensure that new employees receive the information they need.

What is your experience with induction?

In many ways you are like the other employees joining your organisation. You and your company may benefit from the following exercise. The attitudes you experienced during the induction process are likely to be similar to those of other employees. The concerns, if any, which resulted from your induction are likely to be repeated in others.

Carefully think about your initial experiences. Use this process to identify potential ways to improve your induction programme.

	Yes	No
1. I knew how long induction would last.	☐	☐
2. I knew what the induction process would involve.	☐	☐
3. My supervisor/trainer was prepared for induction.	☐	☐
4. All the questions and concerns I had as a new employee were answered during the induction process.	☐	☐
5. I was encouraged to ask questions; and the answers resolved my concerns.	☐	☐
6. Following induction I knew what training programmes would be required and when they would be useful.	☐	☐
7. I felt positive about my new organisation as a result of the induction programme.	☐	☐
8. The peers I met during the induction were friendly and I was encouraged to get to know them.	☐	☐

9. During induction I was provided with the necessary materials. ☐ ☐

10. In retrospect, my induction programme was beneficial. It attained objectives designed to introduce new employees to the job. ☐ ☐

There is a wide range of policies, procedures, activities and other concerns which should be addressed during the induction process. How does a trainer/manager recall what these details are? What can be done to help ensure all employees receive the same information? What can be done to help reduce the time necessary for pre-induction planning?

An induction checklist can be useful for these purposes. There are two basic ways an induction checklist can be developed:

1. Compile those points which must be addressed during induction
2. Develop an employee handbook and distribute it at the time of induction.

A wide range of topics will probably be included in your induction checklist. It is not possible to define each element for every organisation. However, the following list may suggest topics that might be important for your organisation. Consider each carefully. Delete those which are unnecessary and add others that would be helpful during your induction efforts.

Induction checklist

Mark those topics you need to address in your induction programme. Tick topics of importance. If applicable, share the marked list with your manager and then work to develop an improved induction programme which addresses all topics of special concern.

☐ Accidental death insurance

☐ Accidents at work

- [ ] Appearance and dress
- [ ] Attendance
- [ ] Company publications
- [ ] Dental appointments, etc
- [ ] Departmental meetings
- [ ] Disciplinary procedures
- [ ] Educational assistance
- [ ] Emergency procedures
- [ ] Employee opinion survey
- [ ] Employee recognition
- [ ] General meetings
- [ ] Grievance procedures
- [ ] Health and safety
- [ ] Holidays
- [ ] Hours of work
- [ ] Jury duty
- [ ] Leave of absence
- [ ] Lost articles
- [ ] Meals
- [ ] Medical and life insurance
- [ ] Name badges
- [ ] Notice boards
- [ ] Overtime
- [ ] Pay advances
- [ ] Pay days

- ☐ Pay discrepancies and adjustments
- ☐ Pay policy
- ☐ Pay days/Pay periods
- ☐ Pension scheme
- ☐ Performance appraisals
- ☐ Personal property
- ☐ Personnel records
- ☐ Probationary period
- ☐ Recreational and social activities
- ☐ Redundancy policy
- ☐ Seniority
- ☐ Sick leave
- ☐ Sign-in, Sign-out Sheets
- ☐ Standards of conduct
- ☐ Telephone calls
- ☐ Time records
- ☐ Tips
- ☐ Trade union membership and activities
- ☐ Training procedures
- ☐ Uniforms
- ☐ Wage & salary reviews
- ☐ Work schedules
- ☐ Others

Employees: their role in training

Much of the information in this book has concentrated on the trainer. However, the trainer can never forget about the individuals for whom the programme was developed. With today's emphasis on quality service, employees are becoming more involved in how a business operates. Many observers believe this trend will continue and trainees may well be involved in planning training programmes that are most beneficial to them. There are many ways that trainees can be involved as programmes are being planned and implemented. How many can you think of?

Read the following list of ways to involve trainees during the development of training programmes. Tick any procedures currently used in your training programme. Also note those which are not currently used – but which should be.

	In use	**Not in use but needed**
Employees are surveyed about current training needs.	☐	☐
Employees are interviewed about ways that induction schemes can be improved.	☐	☐
Employees evaluate current training programmes and are given an opportunity to comment on how they can be improved.	☐	☐
Training programmes maximise participation by trainees.	☐	☐
Trainees evaluate trainers following each programme.	☐	☐
Trainees evaluate training environment following each programme.	☐	☐
During performance reviews, employees are asked about the relationship between training activities and job requirements and performance.	☐	☐

Recent trainees are solicited to endorse the need for training with their peers. ☐ ☐

Trainees are asked how to improve training during the programme and not just at the conclusion of training. ☐ ☐

CHAPTER 4
Training Resources

Trainers cannot simply sit at their desks to develop training programmes. Even if they could, this is probably not the best way to spend valuable time. Fortunately, there is a wide range of resource material that can be used when developing and conducting training activities. Frequently, this information is available within the trainer's organisation. If this is not the case, other resources should be used such as the public library, or a local university or college.

A wise trainer will not wait until a programme must be developed before relevant information is collected. Instead, resource material should be collected on an ongoing basis. Magazine articles, brochures received through the post, 'interesting' brochures collected at trade shows, etc provide ideas where training resource materials can be found. The sources for excellent training materials are extensive.

Where can I go for help?

Tick each of the training resources identified below which are available for your use. What must you do to begin developing a 'library' of materials for all of your applicable training activities?

Manufacturers' operating manuals (for equipment) ☐

A procedures manual for your organisation ☐

Task breakdowns for jobs within each department ☐

Applicable magazines for your business ☐

- Applicable trade magazines devoted to training, human resource management, etc ☐
- Promotional flyers of training information from training companies ☐
- A list of training schemes from nearby educational institutions ☐
- Libraries available to you ☐
- Membership information in relevant trade associations ☐
- Names and phone numbers of distributor's representatives selling products/equipment/supplies which can be useful during training ☐
- Names and numbers of 'friendly competition' (training ideas gained from those in related businesses) ☐
- 'Canned' training programmes (packaged programmes which present generic training information) ☐
- Names of outside consultants who can be used to teach specific programmes to employees. ☐

There is a wide range of resources available to help trainers develop programmes. Make use of them whenever practical but concentrate your efforts on delivering training programmes – not developing them.

Using visual aids

Nothing is worse than a boring lecture where there is no chance for trainees to become actively involved. Almost as bad is for a trainer to incorporate audio/visual effects into the training programme and do it poorly. Have you ever been in a situation where time was lost and an awkward scene evolved because a slide or film projector would not work, a videotape did not appear on the monitor, or a sound system didn't work?

Part of the preparation for any training activity must be a thorough familiarising with any equipment which is to be used.

Trainers must know how the equipment works and make sure that 'back-up' equipment is available.

You've often heard the question, 'Which came first, the chicken or the egg?' This question can, with revision, be asked as the trainer decides on the role of visual aids in the training programme: 'Which comes first, training programme content or visual aids?'

While we may debate about the first question (the chicken and egg), there can be no debate about the second: content must be determined before visual aids can be selected/developed. This may seem obvious, but many trainers make a mistake. For example, they may find an excellent videotape or a slide presentation dealing with a topic and *then* decide a training programme involving this subject would be helpful. It is far better to decide the content first and then determine how that content should be presented.

While the use of a visual aid may be effective it is also possible that a 'role play', hand-out, on-job demonstration, or other method might be better (and less expensive) than a visual aid. Determine programme content first and then find the best method to present it. Do not use a visual aid unless it is the best technique for delivering the training subject matter or clearly supports the content you are presenting.

None of the information presented in this book will be of use unless it is applied. Your challenge as you have worked through the book has been to consider how the material can be applied to the training activities with which you are involved. We hope this book has caused you to objectively consider ways to improve your training efforts.

The job of a manager is very important. The training responsibilities which you assume as part of that position are significant. You directly affect the lives of your employees and the customers they serve. You have a significant influence on the future success of your organisation. As a 'prepared' trainer you will gain experiences that will help with your own professional growth.

CHAPTER 5
Additional Help

The following pages contain additional activities which were designed to help you apply concepts presented earlier. All forms may be reproduced without further permission.

Task list

You learned about task lists on pages 24–25. To develop a task list, think about your job. Create a list on the form on page 68 for each task you do as part of your job responsibilities. *Be complete.* Ask others who do similar work to analyse your list for additions, deletions, changes. Ask your manager to do the same. You cannot develop a training programme until all tasks for which training is necessary have been defined.

Task list

Your position: ________________________________

Tasks routinely performed in this position include:

1. ________________________________
2. ________________________________
3. ________________________________
4. ________________________________
5. ________________________________
6. ________________________________
7. ________________________________
8. ________________________________
9. ________________________________
10. ________________________________
11. ________________________________
12. ________________________________
13. ________________________________
14. ________________________________
15. ________________________________

Use another sheet of paper if necessary.

Task breakdown

You learned about task breakdowns on page 26. To develop a task breakdown select a task from your list above. Use the form opposite to explain how it should be done. Share your task breakdown with others who do the same task. Is there agreement about the 'how, when, and what' of the task? What problems arise when there is no agreement? What are the implications of any disagreement on the design and conduct of future training programmes?

Task breakdown

Position: ____________________ Task: ____________________

Step	Process	Equipment/Supplies	Other

Use additional paper to continue this analysis if necessary.

Job description

You learned about job descriptions on page 28. Complete the following form for your job. Show it to your boss. What differences, if any, exist in opinions about what your job involves? How can this affect *your* job performance?

Job description

Position: ______________________________

Date of last revision: ___/___/___

1. I report to: ______________________________
2. I supervise: ______________________________
3. Basic tasks which are part of this position are: ____________
   a. ______________________________
   b. ______________________________
   c. ______________________________
   d. ______________________________
   e. ______________________________
   f. ______________________________
   g. ______________________________
   h. ______________________________
4. Equipment which I use includes: ____________________

   ____
5. Personal qualifications important for this job include: ______

   ____
6. Other important aspects of this position are: __________

   ____

   ____

Training plan

Training plan

Use the format below to 'sketch' a training programme you are planning or that your organisation conducts. (It may need to be modified to accommodate your specific requirements.)

Session	Date	Time	Employees Scheduled	Training Objectives	Training Site	Trainer(s)	Equipment/ Supplies	Instructional Method

Training lesson

You learned about training lessons on page 37. Use the format below to develop a training lesson for one task that you regularly do as part of your job. You may wish to select the task for which you developed a task breakdown.

Training lesson

Training topic: ____________________

Training objective(s): ____________________

____

Content of Session	Suggested Activities	Estimated Time Required

Further Reading from Kogan Page

Better Management Skills series

Attacking Absenteeism
Creative Thinking in Business
Delegating for Results
Effective Employee Participation
Effective Meeting Skills
*Effective Performance Appraisals**
Effective Presentation Skills
The Fifty-Minute Supervisor
*How to Communicate Effectively**
*How to Develop a Positive Attitude**
How to Develop Assertiveness
*How to Motivate People**
How to Write a Staff Manual
Improving Relations at Work
Leadership Skills for Women
Learning to Lead
Make Every Minute Count
Managing Disagreement Constructively
Managing Organisational Change
Managing Quality Customer Service
Office Management
Productive Planning
Project Management

* Also available on cassette.

Risk Taking
Self-Managing Teams
Successful Negotiation
Systematic Problem-Solving and Decision Making
Team Building